# OU~~CH!~~

## Behavioural Safety Between The Sheets (Of Paper)

## By G. Milland

Foreword by Robin Evans,
CEO of British Waterways.

Published by Dolman Scott Ltd

ISBN: 978-1-905553-32-7

www.dolmanscott.com

# OUCH!

## Behavioural Safety – Between the sheets (of paper)

### By G. Milland

Disclaimer – The author volunteers the fact that the ideas contained in this book do not represent the official Health & Safety policy, or any policy, of British Waterways.

Additionally he would like it noted that, when Tony Stammers, the Head of Health & Safety for BW, was warned that some of these views might be controversial, he suggested that any fuel for the debate on Behavioural Safety must be aired, regardless of compliance with company policy. Phew.

For the emergency services of the world

Steady the hand of those that can save us from an enraged circumstance,
And ennoble their hearts, lest they ever forget why they do it.

G.Milland

## About the author.

In 1991 Garehoff Milland gave up his attempts to coax large sums of money from the world's business community and retired to realise a childhood dream of becoming a commercial skipper and waterman. In 1997 he joined British Waterways and became a Lock Keeper in 2000.

His wife suggests he should remain unaccustomed to public speaking.

# Contents

# Foreword

Almost everyone who reads this book will have the good fortune to live in a relatively safe environment. Yet hazards are all around us and we are constantly computing what we need to do, or not to do, to avoid the hazards or render them harmless. Despite this natural instinct, accidents do happen. In fact they happen with extraordinary regularity and predictability.

A huge amount has been written about Health & Safety, all of it designed to make us live healthier and safer lives. This book is a welcome addition because it is not written by a theorist, professional or consultant. It is written by an 'ordinary' guy with huge practical experience who sees and hears it as it is. The author draws on this experience and the examples he uses will resonate with us all. It is a no nonsense, practical and simple guide to changing the way we think and behave, to make us and others more aware of the hazards we face, and more capable and willing to overcome them.

Anyone who reads this book will be better equipped and better able to change their own and others behaviour towards safety. That is no small achievement and one that will have long and beneficial effects to us all.

Robin Evans
Chief Executive Officer of British Waterways

# Introduction

Due to a power shortage in 1974 the first ever professional football matches were played on a Sunday in the UK. President Nixon introduced the 55 mph law in America and hands over to President Ford in August. President Pompidou dies of cancer and Juan Peron dies in Argentina aged 78. Britain's first McDonalds fast food restaurant opened in South London and Muhammad Ali proved he's the greatest of all time by beating reigning champion George Foreman and re-claiming his heavyweight title. Beverly Johnson became the first African American to appear on the front cover of Vogue, and in the Caribbean, Grenada celebrated as it gained independence from Great Britain. But much more importantly, some dumb kid steered into me during a really important bike race and I ended up looking like I had a zipper in my head. Oh, and a bunch of politicians passed something called the Health & Safety At Work Act.

Who's this book for?

Quite simply, anybody on or near the ground and those that supervise them. This includes the regular or occasional lone worker. They are their own supervisors.

Because I'm mostly talking about a process of thought as opposed to the technicalities of what and how we 'do' things, it's applicable across any type of working environment, but worth remembering that, from model making to mountaineering, many accidents occur in 'sports' and in our own homes.

# Chapter One

What is Behavioural Safety? How important is Behavioural Safety? Why this book? What are the problems of implementation?

Increasingly since 1974 there have been enough bits of paper entitled 'Thou shalt' and 'Thou shalt not' to give Moses chest pains. But there again a business tycoon (Lord Leverhulme) once lamented that half the money he spent on advertising was wasted. He just wished he knew which half.

From fatality to mild irritation, nobody can deny the decreasing number of accidents. But it's not all due to a large portion of rain forest that's been regurgitated and scribbled on. It's much more subtle than that. The decrease has largely relied on a change in thinking from top to bottom.

Let's face it, Health and Safety has been put at the very top of everybody's agenda using threats and morbid stories. It takes an unusual character to arrive home like an exuberant goal scorer just because they're still breathing or not facing a stretch in the slammer. And most importantly, whether we like it or not, we're all (morally, if not technically) responsible for ourselves and others.

So, this Behavioural Safety business - what is it?

A Health and Safety expert could give you a list as long as your arm. All creditable stuff. I'm afraid my interest is limited to the following few simple points:

1) How we approach and perform an activity safely.

2) How we regularly keep an eye out for a change in our environment.

3) Someone, somewhere, sees something they think is dangerous. The operation is stopped. The observer (or 'facilitator') strikes up a dialogue and they and the 'operator' part on honourable terms. As a result of this intervention an unsafe practice is modified and a possible accident has been prevented.

Simple. Or is it?

How does a green employee tell a wrinkly coffin dodging crane driver that he's operating in an unsafe way? There isn't time to write anything down, dob someone in or grass somebody up. There are, however, years and years to say "If only I'd said the right thing, and in the right sort of way, they might still have had a finger/eye/spleen/job/life...."

Without getting bogged down with the obvious exceptions, everybody has the ability to think effectively. They also have the ability to communicate effectively. They might not know it but they have, and abilities can range from theatrical verbosity to caveman txt mssg spk. This skill can be essential to some aspects of Behavioural Safety, that of, the ability to apply effective communication, using tact and imagery, to stop a potential accident.

How important is Behavioural Safety?

I, like so many other blue collar workers, have had my working life punctuated by risk assessments, method statements, acronyms, mnemonics, training courses, signs with big large red letters saying 'Thou shalt not'…
I knew we all had to go along with all this stuff, but sometimes…oh for goodness sake!!!!!.

Behavioural Safety is much more important than anything I've just mentioned.

All the paperwork etc can be in place and they exist for a reason. At the pink end of the scale, they are there to inform, protect, educate and warn. Somebody has had to try and out think, and subsequently engineer out, any potentially bad happening. If one were to be cynical, they sometimes exist so that someone can say "but all the paperwork was in order." In all technical and 'controlled' industries (petro-chemical, mining etc) hundreds of hours have been spent identifying hazards and minimizing the risks. This is the responsibility of the employer, regardless of how this is achieved.

The same principle applies to our shiny new chainsaw or angle grinder. The manufacturer has gone to great lengths to produce a hand book or manual which points out all the dodgy tricks our new tool will get up to if we let it.

But the bottom line is this. All the signage and paperwork in the world mean absolutely nothing (until a court of enquiry) if our behaviour is not up to the mark.

Where hazards and risks have been identified, we must be made, or make ourselves, aware of what procedures and checks have been put in place. We need to sit down quietly on that pile of boxes that are propping open that fire door and familiarise ourselves with....ah.

Behavioural Safety is the hand that fits inside the Health & Safety glove. Why are they separate? Because Behavioural Safety should occur regardless of paperwork, laws and regulations. The converse is, well, an empty glove.

In the final twenty seconds before an accident, paperwork will not leap out from somewhere and stop an unsafe operation. It's inanimate and doesn't have the power. We do.

Behavioural Safety is everything around and in between everything else. It's the cement that connects precisely laid paving stones or oddly shaped crazy paving.

So, why this book?

From a management perspective, the implementation of Behavioural Safety has two drawbacks.

Firstly, the cost. Training is expensive, and in a sometimes chokingly accountable world, if an investment is to be made its effects have to be quantifiable, which leads directly to the second drawback, that of the difficulties of monitoring and measurement of success.

Massive amounts of paper has been scribbled on expounding the virtues and methods of 'reporting', none of which I could ever denounce, other than to say that some of the procedures I've read about on the internet can get so analytical and scientific they could quickly disappear up their own exhaust pipe and are way beyond me. Other reporting methods relate to critical and highly technical processes and exist out of sheer necessity for the good of all. They're not there just to keep someone in a job.
This is obviously a corporate responsibility in which we can and should participate.

Very simply I'm attempting to set out what I would have liked to have been taught about Behavioural Safety. I would like to have been given a (short) book to read on the subject (in company time?) that had been written by somebody on my (blue collar) level. I would then like to have had regular discussions with my peers, perhaps steered by my supervisor in a team meeting, that would intrigue, stretch, and sometimes amuse me.

It's a budget introduction to what I believe the important aspects of Behavioural Safety are, delivered in the privacy of your own head.

My credentials? None. That should stop any silly questions about letters after my name. It might also infuriate those that do have. Erm, sorry(ish).

The benefits of the successful implementation of Behavioural Safety as a concept to a work force are obvious, especially if one notes a statistic from the Health & Safety Executive.

'Over 80% of accidents result directly from unsafe practice or behaviour'. Other employees within the HSE, but with less of a voice, believe this figure to be 95%.

So, does this mean that this percentage of paperwork was always potentially redundant?

A few years ago some colleagues and I were sent on a different type of course. It changed our thinking forever, but we might have been forgiven for thinking that after two days we would know everything there was to know about Behavioural Safety. Upon reflection the course itself hit a few targets, but missed many others. We spent the majority of our time working on the technique of using tact and imagery when talking to a colleague, to prevent an accident that they may be about to cause.

This is a brief recollection of that course.

The instructor (call me Dave) established his credentials. He was an ex soldier with a bloodied knife, degree in psychology and great sense of humour. He had our full attention. He briefly discussed body language. By the end of this section the girls were sitting demurely as only a pot of honey can, the chaps were sitting as confident as Arnie with gene pools to the wind, and everybody was secretly recording how to come across as a model citizen at the next police interview.

And then came the whammy. How would we, the green employee, tell the wrinkly coffin dodging crane driver that he was operating like a bit of a pillock? He, of course, would inform us that he'd been a Professor of Pillockology for thirty four years and would inquire as to whether our parents were a) as inquisitive and b) indeed, married. Oh dear.

Scary videos and stories

Dave didn't muck about. We got both barrels of yuck and gore. If we'd had the temerity to fall asleep, we would have had nightmares. But there was a different moral to these stories. Yes, written procedures had been put in place, but they lay neatly stacked, largely read but undigested in the metaphorical cab of our nearby truck.

The point was, in each case, there was a fellow employee who could have prevented the accident if only they'd been introduced to the concept of Behavioural Safety.

Role play

"Here's the scenario, now over to you." Oh thanks, Dave. It's alright for you, the charming knife wielding academic who can charismatically run up and down Mount Everest before settling down to a breakfast of six inch nails on unsalted buttered plate washers, confident in the knowledge that, by the end of the day, half the Glaswegian police force would be confessing to a murder that never happened, and the other half thirsting to perform in a ballet. Needless to say Andrew Lloyd Webber would have paid us to keep the day job. Cringe.

By the end of the course I considered what I thought to be a gobsmackingly simple truth about Behavioural Safety. Once one understands what it is, they're well on the way to being able to practise it. "I knew that", we all said by the end of the course. Yes, but so did the lemming to the parachute salesman.

We were now known as facilitators, because, presumably, we could facilitate Behavioural Safety (?)

In defence of the course, there simply wouldn't have been the time (or budget) to cover everything.

So, if the course was an introduction to the subject, then it succeeded. But I wanted more. For instance:-

1) Behaving safely must surely include planning, although if the scale goes from the full blown planning meeting to the 'few minutes beforehand', then I'm tending to dwell on the latter.

2) If we're going to be aware of our working environment with regards to safety, we must be able to increase and improve our powers of observation, especially when it comes to noting a change in conditions.

3) We're all different, and communicate in different ways. There are also thousands of combinations for any given circumstance. You can teach people to trot out standard lines, but wouldn't it be better for them to learn how to come up with their own?

4) If you want to stop an unsafe operation you must first ensure that you're not going to make the operator jump out of his or her skin e.g. with a full revving chainsaw in their hands! You need to stop an operation without endangering anyone, including yourself.

5) What stops us communicating should we see something untoward?

Some of the elements that can inhibit us might be:

Fear or looking like an idiot
Fear of confrontation
Fear of looking like a goody two shoes
Fear of appearing to not behave like a team member
Fear of a clumsy approach to the subject

These very real fears cannot be 'trained' out of somebody on a course. They can, however, be taught to mull over or discuss scenarios (whether fabricated or historic) and imagine how they would deal with it.

6) A missed opportunity

The course could have been used to send out a message to the more experienced (oh alright, old) members of the workforce that, yes, they may have been doing their job for years, but they must now prepare themselves for an approach by someone who is relatively inexperienced. And should this happen, their response should be open and objective.

There is considerable honour in accepting an unpalatable truth that may come 'from the mouths of babes'. I will demonstrate this later when I discuss the old working boatmen who took pride in their ability to learn a new way of working, even if it came from the equivalent of a novice boater.

Effective communication is one of the key factors of Behavioural Safety.

We all already communicate with children, the elderly, spouses, bar staff, pets, etc, and with various degrees of success, use all the tenets of effective communication. By analysing individual methods, and recognising different or new techniques, we could, perhaps, improve the application of Behavioural Safety wherever it's required.

In a perfect environment nobody would have any inhibitions (shyness, lack of confidence or technique etc) about approaching and subsequently 'solving' a situation where somebody, indeed anybody, is behaving in a manner likely to cause injury or death to themselves or others. In other words, everybody becomes a facilitator.

In the case of the lone worker, the process of objectively thinking things through in both the planning stage and actually doing a task should be similar to the team approach.

To digress slightly, I recall as a kid watching a television programme where the presenter (Roy Castle) was attempting to break a world record. He assembled loads of kids in a circle. He asked them to turn their backs on the kid to the right of them. They were now all in a circle facing the back of the person to their left. He then asked them to sit down on the laps of the person they'd just turned their backs on. The circle was self supporting, without beginning or end. I mention this to highlight a collective ideal that we could apply in an industrial and/or societal way. That of watching the backs of others while they in turn watch ours.

A few years ago in a town called Drachten in Holland a 'safety' initiative proposed by a Mr Monderman was given the go ahead. Initially all but three sets of traffic lights were removed. In a town with a population of 50,000, this was a bold move indeed. Miraculously traffic began to flow more smoothly and safely.

Mr Monderman, 61, compared his philosophy of motoring to an ice rink. "Skaters work out things for themselves and it works wonderfully well. I am not an anarchist, but I don't like rules which are ineffective or street furniture that tells people how to behave."

Mr Monderman also said "It works well because it is dangerous, which is exactly what we want. But it shifts the emphasis away from the Government taking the risk, to the driver being responsible for his or her own risk."

The crucial aspect here is that of participation, in this case the residents of Drachten themselves. At the risk of generalising I think the drivers in Milan, Italy, would have their collective work cut out for them, because in my experience the traffic lights there are only a matter of opinion anyway.

# Chapter Two

## *The Basics*

The concepts of Behavioural Safety are very simple. The implications are enormous. The circumstances of where and when they can be applied are infinite to us mere mortals, and so I've tried to identify what I consider to be the big aspects that facilitators (us) need to have taken on board.

1) Observation – The facilitator has an increased awareness of their working environment and the behaviour or actions of self and others.

2) Intervention – The facilitator has mastered their fear of intervening. The fear may still exist, but they're prepared to put their head above the proverbial parapet for the good of others.

3) Communication (or conversation) – The facilitator knows their limits but has also learned a few tricks. This has been achieved by the mental visualisation of, and subsequent working through, imaginary circumstances.

Here's a true story personal to me.

My friend Jill was walking down a busy street in an unfamiliar (English) town. In front of her a man was gripping the wrist (not holding her hand) of a small girl aged about five or six and was dragging her down the road. The girl wasn't hysterical but was

clearly upset. When they turned to cross the road, Jill could hear the little girl saying,
"Where's my mummy, I want my mummy."
The man glanced furtively at Jill before dragging the child across the road.

Jill let the situation pass.

Jill is a completely normal person, just like any of us, in fact.
The story eventually had a happy ending, but it was no thanks to the actions of Jill. More importantly, it was the inactions of Jill which are highly relevant.

Incidentally, she still has nightmares about the implications of this occurrence, none of which need further illustration.

I repeat, this is a true story.

How does this scenario apply to a working environment? How does this apply to a member of a dive team or the office junior at the base camp of a solo arctic explorer?

Simply this:

If you'd intervened and it turned out you were wrong, that's the worst it gets. It may mean you have to take a bit of ribbing/piss-take/verbal aggression. Then so be it. But if you'd been right.....................

Ok, so I've started of with one of the most emotive situations one could encounter. I don't apologise.

Let's look at the factors:

a) Jill was fully aware of the issues of child abduction.
b) She did not hold any relevant rank other than that of a fellow human being.
c) She was, by nature, 'reserved'.
d) She was in a public place.
e) She was on the street for a different purpose other than to catch child abductors.
f) She was female. He was male.
e) She only had a short time to react.
g) She had always striven to avoid personal embarrassment.
h) She was preoccupied with her own world.

Putting yourself in Jill's shoes let's look at the ramifications of action versus inaction.

Action:

Leaving aside for a moment how she could have approached the man, what are the worst and best of outcomes?

1) The man was the legitimate guardian of the child, completely understands your concerns and proceeds to prove his credentials. He also thanks you for your public spirited intervention. To prove

his point further he may involve the child with some nice easy questions.

2) The man was the legitimate guardian of the child and angrily resents your intrusion. He does, however, eventually satisfy you that he and the child are only having a 'pure lemon juice' moment.

3) The man's intentions are not to hurt the child, but is involved in a legal/marital dispute.

4) The man is a child abductor and has been either opportunist or watching a situation carefully for some time. The child faces an unimaginably horrific future.

Later on we can discuss secondary actions to this given scenario, but here is my first and most important point.

You intervened. Not only that, you did so leaving the rights and wrongs, egos and potential embarrassment to be faced after that initial intervention.

Inaction:

In the case of Jill, we may never know. That's haunting.

I'm suggesting that one of the most important aspects of Behavioural Safety is a nurturing of the will to intervene in a situation that's potentially dangerous or harmful to anybody, including ourselves.

In order to nurture this 'will', the potential facilitator (you) will more than likely have to mentally practice. They'll also have to analyse and acknowledge factors which might stop them intervening.

This is why I have deliberately started out with this scenario.

Let's assume that Jill was familiar with the basic tenets of Behavioural Safety. In other words she'd decided action was required.

Let's also give ourselves the luxury of two possible endings.

Observation:

   - Jill was aware of one particularly nasty risk to all children. That of the clever predatory child abductor.

   - On the road to becoming a facilitator she'd read many accounts of how inaction can have the direst of consequences.

   - Jill immediately recognised a potential threat to a colleague (in this case, a young fellow citizen of planet earth).

- Because the consequences of inaction were so abhorrent, she decided the best course of action was...

Intervention

- Despite Jill's self analysis and mental practice she knew she may not get her opening lines right.

- She took into consideration the fact she was in a public place and so in the worst case scenario, physical harm was unlikely to be suffered by her or the child.

- Her decision to intercede, having imagined the worst case scenario, outweighed her natural reserve.

- Having decided that it was safe to intervene and she wasn't going to make the situation worse, she was going to attempt...

Communication

- Jill apologised to the man for what she hoped would be a waste of time.

- She explained that she was concerned that all might not be well, and wouldn't be able to sleep if indeed all wasn't (well) and she'd done nothing.

- She suggested the man would understand, knowing that both a guilty man and a loving father would understand completely.

At this point we'll take the rosiest of scenarios.

- The man explains and convinces Jill he's the legitimate guardian.

- The man congratulates Jill on her spirited behaviour.

- All leave the scene in a contented fashion and with all honour intact.

  and the worst case scenario.

- Through action and words the man convinces Jill that all is not well.
-
- Jill raises the alarm.

- Without putting herself in any unnecessary danger, Jill monitors the situation until a satisfactory conclusion is reached.

NB I don't know about anyone else, but I'd shout for help, follow at a safe practical distance, get on the mobile phone, take license plate details, get physical? Who knows?

In this extreme example, we've mapped the basics of Behavioural Safety onto a given scenario.

To take Behavioural Safety to a community level, the 'Amber Alert' system, initiated in Canada and the US, has, at the time of writing this, helped to save many hundreds of children from an unimaginably horrific future.

Here's a more industrial example. These are the bare bones of another true story.

Bill Morgan worked in a chemical factory. Josh Klein was his close friend and work colleague. Both men were highly experienced in their work and had attended numerous courses relating to Health & Safety. Method statements, risk assessments, signage and decals (diagrammatic symbols) were all in place. Indeed, both men had been very much involved in the procedural set up of their particular operation.

Bill returned after two weeks leave. In his absence Josh had been involved in the planning and implementation of a singular change involving the mixture of certain substances. All the highly detailed paper work was in place. Every precaution had been taken and every eventuality had been catered for. Unless, that is, all this had taken place while you'd been on vacation.

Josh had already started work by the time Bill arrived back at his place of work. Josh saw him set up and waved. He'd go and see Bill in a few minutes. He couldn't stop what he was doing right then because it would take an age to set up again. In a while he'd go and slap Bill on the back, hear about his holidays, tell him about the new procedures, update him on the extension to his house…

BANG!!!!

In a split second Bill's eyes were covered in the corrosive mixture. In less than four seconds, amongst other things, Bill's eye sockets were empty.

The Health & Safety Executive proved in a court of law that there were three guilty parties. Josh Klein was given a suspended jail sentence and the company was made to pay a seven figure fine. Bill Morgan was also told that, if it hadn't been deemed he'd suffered enough, would've also been facing a jail sentence.

The application of Behavioural Safety had not occurred in this instance. It doesn't stop me feeling desperately sorry for the two men. I also wonder if I might have been a Josh Klein or Bill Morgan. Before I'd heard about Jill's story I'm not sure where I would have stood. In both cases, I do now. Knowledge and hindsight are wonderful things.

If Josh and Jill had been made aware of the basic tenets of Behavioural Safety….

Their stories are very different in nature, but all the basic factors could have been applied. I'm suggesting these are observation, intervention and communication.

# Chapter Three

## *Observation*

At the coal face, observation is the first aspect of Behavioural Safety. I'm going to divide it into two main areas - Increased awareness and Pre-emptive. Both divisions have major cross over points, but it's all obvious stuff.

Increased Awareness

For much of the time our surroundings, including our work colleagues, are familiar to us. This could also apply to our garage at home, favourite beach, boat engine room and so on. So many accidents occur because we get so used to a situation and we don't imagine that things can suddenly change. I bet they felt pretty safe on the Titanic.

However safe you feel in your surroundings or performing your chosen activity, think about how so many accidents occur in a place and at a time they've never happened before. It was the first time Captain Smith lost a ship to an iceberg.

But what if, without any increase in effort, we regularly kept an eye out for change? Additionally, what if we took a fresh view of an environment that we've been in a thousand times before?

Walk into, or around, your place of work with a different eye. Imagine what you'd do if there was a fire in the building you're in right now.

Personally I would find being trapped in a fire simply terrifying. I'm as equally terrified of being trapped below the decks of a sinking ship. It's not that I'm some kind of bag of nerves preoccupied with a potential disaster, but more that, in the same way I've arranged where to meet my friends should we get split up at the fun fair, I casually check out fire doors, stairs etc. I'm not doing this at the expense of anything else, I've just activated an awareness button in my head.

Our brains are divided physically and logically. The physical divisions really interest some people, but not me. I do, however, find the logical divisions interesting.

On every computer, if you know how, there is a way one can see all the routines that are either active or waiting in the sidelines of the memory. There's also a whole bunch of other routines asleep on a disk (or equivalent). We can run jobs in the foreground or background. All clever stuff. Even those of us with disorganised minds operate in a similar way, but it's interesting to note that there is a term called 'thrashing'. This is where a computer spends so much time swapping routines in and out, it doesn't get much work done. There are also times when a computer 'freezes'. You can probably imagine, or recall, how these two conditions have either occurred to us or others in the past.

Additionally, there are some who would say that it's technically possible, somehow, for everybody to recall everything they've ever seen or done, heard, smelt or tasted. It's quite spooky to think that we could recall what was written on a road sign we'd read as a child from the back seat of a moving car. In other words, it's all in there, somewhere. We don't carry all this information around with us at the front of our minds. Whether we like it or not it's kept on our 'disc', ready for access (presumably by a hugely expensive hypnotist).

Think about what routines would be going on in your head if you were cycling to work, sucking a boiled sweet, having just had an irritating disagreement with someone at home. Your lottery ticket is in your wallet and in two hours time you have to meet the boss who's got some important news for you. Lots and lots of routines; some in the foreground, some in the background. When you were learning to ride a bike for the first time it took almost all of your brain time. Every now and again you had to remind yourself to breathe. Now you don't think about it, you just do it. The routine is running in the background.

Let's think about some of the other routines that maybe swapping in and out during our cycle ride.

Re-run of an argument (with several successful outcomes, all in your favour)
Traffic awareness
Lottery win shopping list
Route to work
Boiled sweet appreciation and dental guilt
Job security or prospects

The list could go on and on. On the other hand you may keep one routine dominantly in the foreground and let the others fight for lesser places.

Such is the efficiency of our brain we have the capability to go from a day dream to a level of extreme concentration almost instantaneously. All but the most necessary routines would be sent packing if a car suddenly pulled out in front of us.

When we're eating a delicious but bony piece of fish, we've consciously loaded in a caution routine that swaps in and out letting us get on with the crossword puzzle.

The point is we do all this automatically, variously applying different degrees of thought to what routines are needed at any given time for any given task. Some could be called for by 'animal' or instinctive needs and haven't been premeditated (fright, fight and flight). Differing routines would have been used if one has chosen to cook, host, and then appear demure at a dinner party.

Where have these routines come from? A thousand different sources. These include mother nature, our parents or guardians, bitter experience, teachers and training courses. Think of a routine of your own and you can often work out the source. We've probably all met someone who's largely harnessed and designed many of their own routines. As we experience more in life we can modify these routines for ease, speed and effectiveness. On the other side of the coin, some of us don't modify our routines when we should! For example, some people automatically go into an anger routine if just one certain box is ticked, however trivial.

Nobody who's ever studied the mind can ever tell you that you don't have the same potential brain power as Albert Einstein. When it comes to our conscious minds we are like horse riders. Our subconscious minds are like horses (they're actually huge super information processors but stick with me for a bit on this one).

Some people are like Dressage competitors. They are largely in control of all functions of their mind. Even if their horse (the subconscious) occasionally throws them a curved ball, they know how to deal with it.

Then there are those hanging on for dear life to the reins of a runaway racehorse, uncomfortably coming down when the horse is coming up, and showing no immediate signs of being able to control direction or speed.

There are others who are sitting on their incredibly talented race horses but think only of using them to reach the fruit on the upper branches.

How we arrived at the type of relationship with our horse is a job for those that listened at school and are now charging squillions an hour to tell anybody who thinks that they need to know.

I believe that we can make both simple and radical improvements in the way we think, relate to others, achieve, handle anger and disappointments, amuse ourselves and others, give up bad habits, portray ourselves to a potential employer or wealthy wedding guest, and generally improve our futures and the way we go about our daily lives. We can greatly enhance this process by designing our own routines.

If you hadn't noticed I've just tip-toed over an enormous subject. Suffice it to say that we are all 'sitting on top' of a massive processor that can operate at genius level. It can't choose winning lottery numbers but it can solve all sorts of problems for us if we would just design specific routines. After their design and loading these would largely all be running in 'background' mode.

Here's a simple routine I designed for my own personal use.

In my younger days I was never very good at getting up in the morning. Leaving my warm bed in a groggy condition was always going to be an uphill struggle. Every now and again this had caused problems for me and so I designed a little routine. I found a quiet time to visualise myself waking straight up, full of zest for life and excitement at what the day may bring. I also made a bet with my alarm clock that I would do this before it went off. As I set my alarm clock every night I imagine the condition I wish to wake up in and the time that I wish to wake up, mentally saying 'Run wake up (routine)' three times. It took some practice, but after a week I found it had changed my mornings forever.

Unlike us a computer can't forget something unless there's a fault. Our routines, however, need to be kept going like spinning plates. With practice, these routines can kick in without effort and can only increase in their effectiveness.

So how can we greatly increase our powers of observation within our own environment, and with nearly zero extra effort?

Design an awareness routine. Imagine yourself having a greatly enhanced awareness of your surroundings with regards to a potential accident or a change in conditions. You might be in an unfamiliar place, surrounded by unfamiliar activities. Your lack of knowledge may faze you, but it doesn't faze your genius subconscious.

Identify a trigger point. This might be the door to your factory or workshop, door to your vehicle, boat gangplank and so on. It may be a type of location, like any door to a factory, any vehicle door, any boat gangplank. It could also the action of putting on a piece of clothing or equipment.

Two such triggers could be a conscious 'loading' by ourselves when we're in an unfamiliar situation, or the occurrence of a fault we've identified in ourselves and are trying to correct ('I feel my blood beginning to boil. Load calm, adult routine').

The next time you're at your trigger point consciously load your safety awareness routine. Imagine you've walked through a security light beam that can do the triggering for you. With repetition you'll soon find that you've handed this job over to a part of your brain that sorts out the largely automatic aspects of your thought processes.

They say a good amateur pianist practices a piece of music until they can usually get it right, a very good pianist practices until they can get it right all the time, but a concert pianist practices until they can't get it wrong. By the way I'd love to know who 'they' are, because I've got some questions for them.

If you give this a whirl I'm quietly confident that you'll be amazed how quickly it becomes as easy as breathing.

Every now and again you'll find the routine stepping to the front of your conscious mind. It will make you notice, or look differently at, a bit of bared wiring, a trip hazard, a fluid spillage, a frayed rope. A competent craftsperson will tidy up and check all their tools ready for ease of use the next time. Fire fighters and others in similar critical professions, will always keep their equipment clean, tidy and in good order because they exist largely in a world of 'what if?' I'd suggest it's a 'do it right now' state of mind.

Apparently this is a true story. It's now out there in glorious urban myth but worth thinking about.

A man wanted to do some work on the guttering at the back of his house. He needed a harness of some kind. He had a bright (?) idea. He got some rope and walked round to the front of the house where his car was parked on the drive. He then attached the rope to the rear fender and threw the rope over the house. Now he was tied on he could work safely (?) from the top of his ladder.

Bouncing ahead to the end of the story, the first his wife knew about the fact that he was working on the guttering was when she pulled over to let an ambulance overtake her. Only it didn't.

Everyone will have a different opinion on who was the most responsible in this particular case, but I'm going to suggest that an awareness routine will make you notice things that you might consider way outside anything you've previously experienced or have knowledge of. Like a rope attached to the fender of your car, perhaps. And as for his thought processes…

Many professions, such as presidential bodyguards and airline pilots, will have trained hard to achieve a supreme state of constant awareness.

Pre-emptive observation

Pre-emptive observation can further be broadly sub divided.

1)  People around us
2)  Changing conditions

What if we regularly took a look at our colleague working a short distance away from us. Has anything changed since they started working which you think they might not have seen?

Before we go any further on this one there might be a tendency for us to look upon this concept as being nosey, spying or furtive. To dispel this I would wish to remind you of the self supporting circle. In a perfect world everybody should be self supporting in any activity and as much as you are keeping an eye out for others, they'll be keeping an eye out for you.

Some equipment use severely limits our senses, as can general background noise. Concentration on a difficult mental task can do the same.

Without trying to limit the number of scenarios let's look at a range of circumstances one might have spotted with their heightened sense of awareness.

A shoelace has come undone.
A lanyard would snag or 'give' should it be needed.
A warning light has activated.
A piece of equipment has started to smoulder.
Liquid is pooling on the floor.
An item of PPE (Personal Protective Equipment) has failed.
A squall has appeared on the horizon behind us.
A nut is vibrating loose on a bolt.
A beam or girder has started to show signs of undue stress.
A curious person has entered a dangerous working zone.
Someone has stopped using a piece of equipment and now doesn't look too steady on their feet.
An equipment safety guard is missing or damaged.
Sparks from a grinder are landing where they shouldn't.
Sunburn.

Again the list is seemingly endless.

Then we come to one of the most important aspects of observation.

You see someone who either is, or you suspect is, operating in an unsafe way.

They may be doing this for several different reasons.

Lack of training.
Having fun(!!)
In a hurry.
Ignoring others that are too close by.
A complete lack of planning.
Doing something in the easiest way,

and so on.

Someone, who has never suffered with a bad back, is about to lift something heavy in the wrong way and without 'kicking' or testing the weight. This is an obvious one, but in less obvious circumstances you may be wrong (but you're going to pursue it further anyway).

The important thing is we've spotted a hazard, change or possible unsafe behaviour. This is because of our new heightened sense of awareness in our environment and of those operating around us.

Some people are in professions that have required many hundreds of hours of practice and planning. They have attained their level of competence because they've been shown, or taught to think about, worst case scenarios. Most of us are not required to do so. But...somebody next to you is using a lethally sharp blade to open the packaging of their long awaited new computer...that tide is going to be coming in really quickly, really soon…the tyre on that forklift truck looks a bit damaged or low…etc

Like a chess player thinking many moves ahead, pre-emptive observation is where you've spotted a potential accident while it's still a dot on the horizon. The size of these dots can vary. An incomplete First Aid kit can be both a large or small dot depending on where it's required (ok, First Aid kits are always important but I'm talking about the difference between a public library and a combat situation). I'd suggest a pile of boxes keeping open a fire retardant door or blocking a fire escape is a large dot. Once your dot has been identified you can act upon it.

As a final note on observation I've quickly found that my heightened awareness routine began to run all day and required no effort. I note it kicking in and out when I'm driving, boating, in the pub, using tools, playing with the kids etc. It even works as I write chastely from my hospital bed (oops!)

# Chapter Four

## *Intervention*

Intervention, like all the basic tenets of Behavioural Safety, is wide ranging in terms of possible or necessary participation. In the same way that observation merges into intervention, intervention merges into communication.

Whether or not you intervene is going to depend entirely on an initial rapid assessment (the stitching on the crane strop supporting the boat is ripping and is on the crane driver's blind side, but we're only out walking the dog) or the observation of a changing circumstance (the breeze is slowly backing and might well soon be blowing offshore, possibly endangering the kids playing just beyond the surf in that toy dinghy, but they're not our kids and the parents don't seem too bothered).

That decision is also going to be based on the worst case scenario of you not acting at all. We've already heard about Jill and the potential child abduction, and I'd like to think that anybody, once familiar with the circumstances, would intervene (or take action) every time. At this extreme end of the scale the only problems to overcome concern ourselves. Most of us hate confrontation. Most of us don't know what we'd say. We can have a look at this later.

Let's look at the smallest and largest of possibilities, from the opening of the computer box with a sharp knife, to the sinking of the Titanic.

1) Within the boundaries of pre-emptive observation you've become aware that a big box has arrived in your busy office. A colleague is setting about opening the box using a sharp blade. The blade is the perfect tool for the job and the sensible colleague isn't displaying the near hysterical excitement of a kid at Christmas, but wants the job over with quickly. You've sustained a severe cut under similar circumstances in the past. It may be enough just to note that the operation is happening and you're there to help should anything untoward occur. On the other hand you may want to remind the operator (perhaps light heartedly) just what that knife did to you.

2) According to James Cameron's version of the sinking of the Titanic, to further boost the prestige of the ship, both Captain Smith and J. Bruce Ismay (passenger and President of the company that owned the ship) had arranged with the Chief Engineer to 'put the pedal to the metal' for a few hours during the maiden voyage between Queenstown and New York. They all knew of the iceberg warnings. If this version of events was true, one would like to think that after the ship had struck the iceberg, an exchange had occurred between Ismay and Smith along the lines of 'we didn't really think that one through.' Also, back on dry land, I wonder how many times Mrs Ismay said "Yes

dearest, but hindsight's a wonderful thing. Now please do try and get some sleep."

What are the factors that stop intervention?

Maybe we think that:

a) The chances of a particular series of events turning sour are ridiculously minimal.
b) We're too busy.
c) We've no knowledge or experience of the observed activity.
d) We've never really got on with the 'operator'.
e) We wouldn't know what to say.
f) We don't want to put ourselves at risk by entering a dangerous zone.
g) We're surrounded by people or colleagues and don't wish to appear foolish or naïve.
h) We've too much respect for the 'operator's' experience and expertise.
i) We're not going to be responsible for other kids when their parents are so close by.
j) We can't believe we're the only ones to have seen the obvious change in our environmental conditions/beam strain/pulled anchor bolt.
k) We can't go to lunch/home until they've finished what they're doing.
l) We've intervened before but the operator is still behaving in an unsafe way,

and so on.

I'm deliberately mixing recreational, domestic and industrial examples together, because, although you may be an extremely skilled fighter pilot, we still all have to go home and mow the lawn, get kites out of trees, do a bit of free format rock climbing etc.

The intervention aspect of Behavioural Safety has two darker implications.

1)   The personal consequences of inaction.
2)   The legal consequences of inaction.

Let's look at the first one.

Ask yourself some questions. Are you the kind of person who believes that an accident or misfortune to others can be either deserved or an act of God? If I read in a newspaper about a house burglar who's broken his ankle after falling from a roof, I can't feel myself sympathising with their pain. Mind you these days they'd probably sue the homeowner for not providing proper signage, decent surfacing, PPE, providing a proper method statement and risk assessment. I just hope the lawyer who takes this kind of case on gets their home burgled regularly.

I'm not going to dwell too much on this one because, in the same way we do things for a reason, we also don't do things for a reason. We're all different. Suffice it to say that Jill felt awful but got off lightly, and J. B Ismay died a broken man.

There are also a surprising number of people who believe in 'what goes around comes around'. This may be worth thinking about when it comes to mutual support (observation, intervention etc.)

I've never fully understood those that say they have no regrets. I have loads. Their memory can make me wince with varying degrees of severity and at any time during my waking hours. Sometimes thought, sometimes word, sometimes deed (which includes inaction.) I do, however, regret my regrets, and to that end (and for largely selfish reasons) strive to stop the list getting any longer.

And the second one.

The consequences of inaction can have very serious legal implications. The bottom line is this. If you were operating in a controlled environment and a court of enquiry can prove that you were negligently inactive in not aiding the prevention of an injury or fatality, you are seriously facing the possibility of a large fine or maybe a prison sentence.

There is a difference, and yet similarities, between intervention and a straightforward rescue. Thankfully there are many men and women who train hard in various disciplines so that they can save us from an enraged circumstance without worsening the situation. Suffice it to say an out and out rescue requires that extra few seconds of thinking time so as to ensure we aren't going to make the situation worse.

For instance, a drowning person will undoubtedly use you as buoyancy at your expense and a person in the throes of electrocution will happily pass on their predicament to you should you touch them. But if my kids were trapped in a burning building…

Every one of us would have our own way of dealing with, or reacting to, an emergency.

In a perfect world proactive Behavioural Safety would have negated the need for a rescue in a large percentage of cases, purely because of observation, intervention and communication.

A cross over point between intervention and communication is how and when it's safe to intervene.

If, when I'm using a brush cutter or a chainsaw in the garden, one of my kids needs to show me a crucially important bug in a jam jar, they know not to come and tap me on the shoulder. They will either make a wide safe circle until they're in my vision, or they'll throw something in my direction where I could see it. This is open to abuse if you've just had an argument with your teenagers so hide any half bricks that might be lying around.

These days a crane operation usually requires a 'slinger' or 'banksman' in addition to the crane operator. A slinger is the eyes and ears of the crane operator and essentially in charge of 'the lift'. They can either communicate with two-way radios or hand signals. There are a few of the hand signals that could be used in any situation. For example,

Stop (temporarily) – Raised palm of one hand facing the operator.
Stop (completely or quickly) – Two raised palms facing the operator.
Raise – index finger pointing up, rotating
Lower – index finger pointing down, rotating

From lowering grand pianos to stopping a vehicle, these might be useful in a noisy environment or at a distance.

There's also the good old tried and tested method of whistling.

Now we've intervened we've got to communicate.

# Chapter Five

## *Some ways in which we communicate*

Communication is an enormous and fascinating subject. It ranges from the tiniest finger movement of the semi comatosed, to Martin Luther King's powerful and moving 'I have a dream' speech, and from the first cry of the new born baby to the "Houston, we have a problem."

It also exists as pictures and diagrams, literature, music, fashions and emotional expressions etc. Curiously its lack of use can produce the same results as its effective use, in that no communication at all can cause wars, divorces and accidents, amongst other things. Sometimes just a few words have the power to permanently damage or inspire young minds. Where, how and when we communicate can be an awesome responsibility, and yet so often we are careless and lazy with this loaded gun. Similarly, acknowledgement, or not, of somebody's presence can make or break their day. Sometimes, the absence of communication is a form of communication in its own right.

Have a bit of a breather.

I used to write Lockeeper stories, and here's one about inactive communication.

~~~

Loyalty is a curious thing. I seem to remember during some American/Arab negotiations about

Saddam Hussein, somebody on the Arab side said 'he may be a sonoffabitch, but he's <u>our</u> sonoffabitch'.

I'd previously come to the conclusion that God hates waste. People on boats can do gobsmackingly funny things, especially when they go through locks. The locks are often in the middle of nowhere and it's a tragic shame that so much mirth is wasted because it goes un-witnessed.

And so God invented the Lockeeper.

I think it was a Tuesday. It had been a beautiful summer day and I'd been up river doing Lockeepy type things. Mrs Lockeeper had spent the day doing Mrs Lockeepy type things and would normally have been in her usual good natured mood that can only be darkened by a few cubic inches of plastic explosive, or me.

I arrived home and took my place next to Mrs Lockeeper on the patio, ready to enjoy our ritual of tea and banter, which generally involved me trying to persuade her that I worked hard for a living. But whilst I'd been away she'd encountered a rather unpleasant situation.

Just after lunch Mrs Lockeeper had been shearing one of the children on the patio and was interrupted by some shouting.
"Where's the Lockeeper!! This paddle gear doesn't work". After several renditions of this and other variations on the theme, Mrs Lockeeper went down

to the source of the noise which turned out to be a family on a wide beam hire boat, enjoying a day trip. Or not. She encountered one of the most dangerous scenarios one can ever get on a river or canal. Somebody who once knew somebody else who'd purchased a parrot from someone's second cousin who'd once bumped into somebody else who'd once seen a boat from a great distance, and therefore knew everything there was to know about boating. In this case it was the matriarch of the tribe.

Mrs Lockeeper patiently explained how to use the paddle gear but encountered such rudeness she almost had to resort to riding off on John, the Spanish horse (went off on Juan). This was the news that welcomed me back to the fold. Armed with the knowledge that it was only a day hire, what goes up river must come down river. I did what any other full bloodied and fearless Lockeeper would do when someone was rude to their wife. I prepared to dead-head the marigolds.

Two paths lead down from the house to the lock, both lined on either side with a total of one hundred and ninety two marigold plants. In times of crisis, America has a large arsenal of nuclear weapons and a loud hailer, China has about a billion soldiers and most British people put the kettle on. But I have my marigolds.

Later that afternoon the familiar wide beam hire boat approached the lock. Dad and the two teenage kids were standing on the fore deck of the boat ready to disembark. A steady stream of orders was coming from the back of the boat courtesy of a black hole with earrings. I got into position and prepared the ambush.

Commercial boat people will rarely comment on other people's boat handling, employing the much more powerful insult of saying nothing at all and in some severe cases, utilising nothing more than a dark 'category five' stare. I started at the top of one of the paths and began my calm and methodical assault towards Frau Hitler's ego. She'd been rude to my wife. The boat was in the lock. As so often happens when somebody on a boat wants to announce their credentials, a demonstration of expertise was required for my benefit. The Frau started a loud delivery on how not to hang up a boat in a lock. This should be good, I told the marigolds, as the exquisitely maintained paddle gear was wound up. Being merely a 'correctional' lock it only had a rise and fall of about eighteen inches, so there was no danger of me having to break my Trappist silence.

They hung up the boat. I couldn't have done a better job myself of getting it oh so horribly wrong.

The pressure was really on as I got halfway down the path and still resolutely refused to look at them. The lock was re flooded amid shouts, screams and curses. Still the orders came thick and fast, but the Frau's voice was beginning to crack under the pressure of my relentless dead-heading. The water was let out of the lock and a gate was opened. Just the one gate. It was a wide beam boat. You need to open two gates for a wide beam. She must have been in a hurry. She'd been rude to my wife. With only a few marigolds left I heard the engine revved hard and waited for the bang. I had to watch. Afterwards she went down inside the boat to get on with some embroidery because the crew were very convincing with their threats. I had no sympathy. She'd been rude to my wife. Loyalty is a funny thing.

~~~

Things start getting really complex when we look at the way we say words. Not only the choice and mixture, but intonation, inflection and volume, all add colour to our utterances.

There's also unintentional communication. This can be simple body language or the actions of someone who is trying to appear clever and achieving the complete opposite.

Something as simple as a smile can be misinterpreted.

Sign language was being used for thousands of years before the author of the first Greek tragedy got depressed, and is still developing today. It's interesting to note that in some countries, if you actually mean to signal to someone that something is 'ok' or good by joining the tip of your index finger with the tip of you thumb, you might just be informing them that they do, in fact, resemble the less fragrant end of the human form.

People communicate in different ways, and we all further vary our communication according to whom we're talking.

Some people are highly talented when passing on ideas or knowledge, telling a joke, or conveying authority. Others have difficulty with brain to mouth coordination and we've all, at some time, let our foot get in between. There are many different reasons for this range in ability, but there is no doubt in my mind that much of it is down to a 'fitness'. A child that's grown up with many noisy boisterous siblings, or has had to think on their feet to survive, will have undoubtedly learned a trick or two about fast and effective communication.

Somebody who makes their living from talking on their feet (a stand-up comedian or a politician, for example) will practice for hours on end, mentally formulating words and phrases. To a certain extent, with reference to Behavioural Safety, we can do the same.

I don't know about anyone else, but the thought of getting up in front of anyone, especially my work colleagues and participating in role play fills me with dread. When this has happened in the past, the 'leader' would have found me attempting to tread on my own hands rather than volunteer.

I'm going to divide our possible need to communicate into two sections.

1)    Pre-emptive Communications

2)    Imperative Communications

Pre-emptive communication is used when we are about to commence a job, plan a journey, feel the need to talk or think about a possible change in our plans etc.

Imperative communication is where we simply have to communicate quickly in order to prevent a possible accident.

Ultimately I'm going to suggest that we get to a stage where we can practice mentally what we'd say and do in any situation relative to our work place or activity. (Incidentally, I'm still finalizing what I'd do in the Jill/abductor situation). In order to get there I'm going to take a circuitous, but hopefully interesting, route.

Body language is another large and fascinating subject. The fact that we communicate our thoughts and feelings by how we unconsciously 'signal' with our bodies is scary. For most of us it's not an exact science. I remember being accused of taking a defensive and negative stance (I had my arms crossed), when in fact I was just a bit chilly. But I think it's relevant, especially when one realises that, not only would it be useful to observe other people's body language if we've felt the need to approach them, but we could well be about to portray a beacon of fear, aggression or uncertainty ourselves.

Let's remind ourselves of a few of the basics.
Prefix all of the below with 'it could mean'.

Folded arms
  – cautious, negative or defensive (or just chilly)

Arm across body, elbow resting on the arm at ninety degrees and chin in palm
  – negative, disdain, critical of the other person.

Looking over the rim of glasses or head slightly angled down and looking up (at you)
  -   attempt to display superior knowledge or disbelief.

Pinching bridge of nose
  -   deep thought or concern.

Rubbing nose.
  -   conveying doubt or negative reaction.

Feet on desk
  -   secure of territory and self confidence

Shoulders back and/or inflated chest
  -   aggression, suppressed anger, physical readiness, or simply been ordered to by a sergeant

Fixed eye contact

- Can range from abject hatred to great interest

Relaxed brow and eyes
- Comfortable with information or situation.

Avoidance of, or furtive, eye contact
- Lying, guilt, disinterest or emotionally defensive

Furrowed Brow (without smile)
- Tension, fear, confusion

Shoulders hunched forward
- Feeling inferior or disinterested

Finger tapping
- Impatience, anxiety or boredom

Leaning forward
- Attentive, interested

Adopting your stance
- Wants to relate to you (unless you're being aggressive)

Quick short inhalations
- Anxiety or anger

A smile that lasts too long, or disappears too quickly
- Fake!

Rapid nodding
- Excitable agreement and wants to contribute

Slow nodding
- Processing information carefully or encouraging you

Unnecessary collar rubbing or tie adjustment
- Nervous or insecure

Pursed lips
- Disapproval or disagreement from a fixed point of view

Lip biting
- Insecurity, embarrassment or guilt

Hand covering, or fingers playing with, mouth
- Get ready for an untruth.

Hands steepled to face or chin
- Indicates intellect or the intelligent processing of information

Open hands
- Sincere or open to ideas

Covered, or overlaying, hands
- Barrier building, concealing insecurity or feelings

Clasping hands
- Defensive

Clenched Fist
- Apart from the obvious threatening gesture, anger or irritation

Weak handshake
- Shy, nervous, doesn't really want to interact

Firm handshake
- Confident, open, happy to interact. With handshakes it's all in the willingness to touch palms.

Palm down handshake
- Wishes to dominate

Palm up handshake
- Wishes to offer support

For right handed people:
Looking up and left when giving information
- Creating or fabricating
Looking up and right
- Recalling an event or a truth

There are hundreds of these examples, especially when one thinks about all the different combinations of their use. I've again tip - toed over a big subject but I do think it can have relevance to Behavioural Safety. For example, if you've confronted someone, your observation of their body language could contribute to how you pursue the conversation. It could also inform you as to how that person is feeling at the end of your conversation e.g. if they're smiling kindly at you with clenched fists…!

Maybe, more importantly, on the basis that much of our observation is subconscious, what are we communicating with our own body language? Are we, perhaps, coming across as nervous, caring, intelligent, deceitful or obnoxious?

Another fascinating subject relating to how we communicate is that of Transactional Analysis. It sounds a bit technical but the basics are, well, basic.

In the mid 1960's, Dr Eric Berne produced a book entitled 'Games People Play'. It still sells by the truckload today. In a nutshell he'd worked out a way of identifying and referencing how we interact and communicate with each other. I'll attempt to put a cubic ton into a matchbox.

We can all operate on three different levels. Another way to put it is that we have three ego states. Parent, adult and child.

Parent – The parent state is when we use what we have learned from our parents, guardians, teachers etc.
This state can be further divided into two. The first is the nurturing parent ("Of course you can watch the end of the film, even though it's bed time. It's quite educational")
The second is the critical parent ("I don't care what's on telly, it's bed time now! Because I said so!!")

Adult – This state is our most rational. It's when we accurately process all the information from the circumstances around us, evaluate, and then act upon our logical, unprejudiced conclusions (I'm going to be a little more tired tomorrow, but the extra information I'm going to gain from staying up to watch the end of the programme will be worth it).

Child – The child state can be looked on as a memory bank of our childhood experiences and memories. This state can be further divided into three.

The free child ("Oh please let me stay up to watch the end of the programme. I'm finding it really interesting and I'll be double, double good tomorrow with extra cream on top. By the way, your hair looks nice").

The adapted child ("I really would like to stay up a little longer, but if you really insist I'll be good and do what you say. If I really must").

The rebellious child ("£$%^ your telly, $%£^ your bed time rule and £$%^ you!!")

In a Behavioural Safety context, somebody's initial reaction (thoughts if not words) to your spirited intervention might be:

Parent - Don't you try and tell me I'm operating in an unsafe way. I've been operating this way for years and I know better. If you'd my experience then you'd realise what you're suggesting is ludicrous.

Or
Adult - I'm just going to take some time out to listen to your fears and then explain to you the checks I've identified. If you're right, I'll hold up my hands, if not, I'll attempt to explain them to you (up to a point).

Or

Child - Piss off, numpty, I'm busy. Oh and by the way, you've got a really big nose.

With a little practice one can quickly identify where somebody is 'coming from'. This applies to any conversation with anyone, anytime.

When it comes to practising our relevant creative imagery, e.g. imagining a circumstance in our working environment or activity where we're intervening to stop a potential accident, it is imperative that we operate from an adult ego state, even if we feel cross, or are experiencing a rising sense of panic. From this ego state one can rapidly stop a potentially dangerous activity, communicate your concerns effectively, and stand the best chance of allowing everyone concerned to 'leave the field' with all honour intact. Operating from either a parent or child state will probably push all the corresponding buttons in the other persons head, greatly diminishing your power and right to say something to anyone, anytime.

For example:

Parent - "Stop what you're doing right now, you stupid idiot!!"
 - "Have you no idea what could happen if you carry on like that?"
 - "Are you blind? Couldn't you see those people in your safety zone?"

Child -   "If you don't stop right now I'm going to scream and scream and scream until I'm sick".

So to recap:

We've absorbed a little knowledge of body language. This could help us to identify how a person is reacting to our 'interference'. Remembering that they don't know what we're going to say, our body language is going to be benign and unthreatening, but not timid or insecure.

We are going to communicate in an adult way. We may not be in full possession of the facts or have any experience of the operation or activity, but we feel that something isn't right. Regardless of which ego state the operator responds with, we are going to remain in this adult state.

What is the adult ego state again?

It's our sensible head. It can process information in any form and can calculate a sensible conclusion as to how to proceed with either action or communication. It is not open to emotional outbursts from either of the other states (parent or child). It is ultimately unselfish. It is able to communicate a desire to learn, or able to pass on extra information from an unprejudiced view point. In the context of Behavioural Safety, its only desire is the safety and well-being of self and others. The adult state is not restricted to age. A ten year old kid can communicate as an adult while their cantankerous octogenarian grandpa can play the child.

Just to take a break for a moment, what a wonderfully improved world we could live in if everybody operated, or was brought up to operate in, the adult ego state at all times. From the centre of a disaster area to domestic strife, and from global political decision making to playing a game of marbles.

One important aspect of communication (defined within Transactional Analysis) is that of 'strokes'.

Very simply, Eric Berne defined a stroke as a 'unit of human recognition'. A stroke can be given by any form of human communication e.g. a smile, a word, a touch etc.
Strokes can be both negative and positive, and most of us would much rather receive an "I like you" than an "I don't like you." As children, if we can't get enough positive strokes then we'll go for the negative ones, because a negative stroke is better than no stroke at all. I'm sure we've all come across

people of all ages who deliberately irritate us because they would rather do that than be ignored.

Strokes can further be divided into two forms.

Conditional strokes - These are given to us for what we do, good or bad. ("That was really helpful/bloody stupid")

Unconditional strokes - These are given to us just for being ("Who's an ickle scrummy wummy baby den?", "The fact that you exist really lights up my life/really gets me down".)

The strokes we receive as kids can certainly have a great bearing on how we view ourselves and those around us and it's another loaded gun that we can sometimes be so careless with.

With Behavioural Safety we can search for a positive stroke to aid our entry into a conversation that nobody actually wants to have. Unless of course it's an emergency, in which case the nice strokes are going to have to wait a bit. Even then, they're still important in the secondary stages!

Whilst it might often be possible to compliment someone on their clean machine, sharp tools, cool hat, powerful engine, new carabiners, physical strength, body piercing (?) etc, we may have to resort to a watered down version of a positive stroke. "You look tired/wet/as if you're having fun" etc. In other words, you've noticed their condition and therefore have acknowledged and positively empathised with them.

In addition to the stroke, to start a conversation using a totally unrelated subject to what you want to talk about is also positive. It might be the weather, where you've walked from or it maybe an innocent question about the job. But you've established communication on an equal, non combative footing.

# Chapter 6

## *Communication - What we might say*

The next section is about how or what we could say next.

We've seen something or an action that we suspect is going to cause injury to the operator, ourselves or somebody standing close by. Our aim is to communicate effectively, thereby stopping the activity and doing so in such a way, that the operator will modify their behaviour in the future. This is going to take some practice and I'm suggesting that the best way to practice is to invent any scenario that you might possibly (sometimes almost impossibly) encounter in your world. Go mad, think outside the box. There are no rules because it's your imagination. The upside is that you get to play the hero.

Whether it be loved ones or work colleagues, only you know about the relationships you have around you. Only you know how easy, or hard, you find it to communicate with strangers. Also, communicating with a big dominant personality can often be a problem for many of us graduates from the 'School of Church Mice'.

How many times have we had a disagreement with someone and afterwards said to ourselves 'if only I'd said this or that'. Being wise after the event and having the benefit of hindsight are important to our learning. So what if we strive to get wise before the event?

What I'm actually suggesting is role play but without the witnesses. Having said that, a discussion of ideas within a team meeting might be just as effective.

You've now opened up communications and the initiative for the next step in the conversation is yours. Let's look at an array of circumstances, some easier than others.

-You've been doing your job for several years but somebody inexperienced is operating around you in an unsafe way.

-You've only been operating for a few weeks, but somebody who's been in the job for years is putting themselves, you, or others at risk.

- You're on a beach and you've noticed a change in conditions that could possibly, but dramatically, affect the welfare of somebody else's kids.

- You're out with a climbing team. You've noticed deterioration in the condition of one of your fellows, but they don't want to be the one to spoil the fun.

- The job is just one quick cut with a chain saw or a grinder. Your colleague can't be bothered to put on all that silly protective equipment.

- You're in a demolition team and the duration of the job would be greatly reduced by cutting the wrong beam followed by a bit of long legged leaping.

- You're at a quay side and some people have just bought a new boat. You've noticed, by the way that they're struggling to slip the craft, that they're complete novices. The sky off the coast looks black.

- One of your work colleagues is 'riding' a co-worker too hard for no apparent reason and making their lives a misery. They dread coming to work.

- You're in a team, all of equal rank. The team have just completed a rapid planning session that has, in your opinion, missed a major safety factor or 'what if'? The team is about to disband but you are not the most experienced or outspoken member of that team.

- Somebody has handed someone else a gun for them to admire or use. The gun is unchecked but thought to be unloaded. Rules for such an exchange have been ignored.

- Whilst you're not a crane operator or slinger yourself, a concrete hopper is about to be emptied into a confined space with men working in it. No concession has been made for jib bend.

- A friend of yours wants to fell a tree in their garden using an old chainsaw. They have no training, no protective equipment, but they're excited at the prospect as well as having a very playful dog.

- You're part of a gang who have to dig a hole. Someone has forgotten the CAT Scanner (detects electrical cable etc). It's a long way back to get it.

- Somebody's about to pick something up that's either possibly beyond their capabilities, or not using the correct lifting technique,

and so on.

Every circumstance is going to be different, which is why you're going to have to tailor your 'practice' to your own specific environment. You might find it useful to test your own communication 'skill base' e.g. what would it be in character to say and what might be totally out of character (but you might need to say it anyway)?

On the Behavioural Safety course I mentioned earlier, we were told (during role play, cringe) to experiment along the lines of "…and so how would your wife/loved one/kids/mum feel if you were to eventually arrive home with no eyes/spleen/leg or job/chance of avoiding a prison term?"

Yes, this is a powerful tack and I've certainly started taking a long hard look at my own activities since playing with the kids became so much fun. But it's not 'one size fits all'.

Let's go for the Behavioural Safety throat. We can bypass the strokes etc, but we must never bypass our 'intervention' ideals (are we going to make the operator jump out of their skin or make the situation worse by our method?)

(Raise both hands) "Stop, that's unsafe"

It doesn't matter how long either you, or they, have been in the job, what kind of danger there is (bad practice or a change in conditions), this will stop the activity.

Even if you have a speech impediment, suffer from acute shyness or are physically terrified, this simple line and signage will work. It is like jumping off a high diving board. The main thing is you've stopped what you have perceived to be a dangerous action.

It differs from "Don't you think that's dangerous?" or "That looks dangerous to me." These lines may be more appropriate in numerous circumstances but we have to understand the difference. The first either is, or verging on, a command. The latter are invitations for a discussion.

Things get easier (up to a point) when it comes to pointing out a change in conditions.

Having spoken of your concern to the operator, they might do or say one of three things.

1) "Phew, thanks. I hadn't noticed that!"
2) "What? No I hadn't noticed that, but it'll be OK and I'm going to carry on anyway."
3) "Yes, I'd noticed that, but it's not dangerous.

If you're not satisfied with either of the second two answers, you might now have to create a picture in their minds of the worst case scenario. We'll come back to this.

Here's a story that moves the goal posts a little.

Early one morning a friend of mine was driving through the city of Bath. A man was using a tall extendable ladder to clean the windows on the upper floors of an office building. The base of his ladder was out in the road that was soon to become very busy. There were no visible markers or warnings to the vehicle drivers. All they could see, if they were totally concentrating, was the line of a ladder side on. My friend pulled over and parked half on the pavement, half on the road before putting on his hazard lights. The next time the man came down to move the ladder my friend said to him,

"Hello, mate. Where to next?"

"What do you mean?" said our cleaning mountaineer.

"You move your ladder, and then I'll know where to move the car," he replied cheerfully.

"What for?"

"To protect you from drivers like me," came the answer.

My friend then proceeded to paint a picture of what would have happened if he'd been in the large truck he'd have normally been driving, the physical pain of two of broken legs, the loss of job, earnings and a probable visit from some seriously curious officials.

Yes, he further explained, it may have taken an extreme long shot for his truck to take out the bottom of the ladder, but it was still a chance. There are stations to be changed on the radio, distractions on the other side of the road to be noticed, sneezing fits to be enjoyed, tyres to burst, overtaking motorbikes to be avoided, windscreens to be squirted clean etc. Moreover, the chances of an accident could have been further reduced if the window cleaner had put something highly visible around the base of the ladder.

At this point it's probably worth mentioning that there is a good chance you are going to have to go out of your own way, or lend a hand, to stop an accident happening. My friend didn't want to prolong his journey, but also would have hated reading about the window cleaner's possibly fatal accident in the papers the next day. He had to do something about it simply because he had seen it. His boss totally understood his lateness. I don't think my friend would have cared too much if he hadn't. He knew he'd done the right thing.

There again some might say 'it's not my problem if he's stupid enough to get hurt like that'. Mmmm. Self supporting circle? What about their own backs being watched in, perhaps, less stupid circumstances?

One of the most difficult situations can be when a relatively inexperienced worker sees a more seasoned operator working or acting unsafely.

"Go away, you're just a puppy, where as I've been doing this for years".

At this stage it might be a good time to ask ourselves a question.
How would I respond to such an interruption? Would I baulk at the temerity of some young

whipper snapper daring to criticize my way of working? Will I snap back from a parent or child ego state? Or would I remember the adult ego state? Let's hope we'd respond in the best way.

'I'm only human and may have missed something'.
"OK, fire away; what do you think is the problem? You could be right."

or

'I think I know what their concern is, but it wouldn't hurt either of us to clarify the way I've arrived at my mode of operation'.
"OK, you're right to have mentioned it and this is what I've done to minimise any risk. See that fire extinguisher/gas detector /signage/COSHH assessment over there...?"

There are always new ideas and new ways of doing things. I'd been picking up dead rats by their tails for years until somebody pointed out that, with reference to Weils Disease, a rat's tail is the dirtiest part of the body because a rat has a pee and then moves forward. Yes, I used protective gloves, but what else did I touch with those gloves that I may later touch with my bare hands?

Moving freight around the inland waterways was a major contribution to the industrial revolution in the UK. From the mid 18th Century to the 1960s, the families that worked these boats (either a butty towed by a horse, or two boats working together as a motor boat and butty) had perfected their craft over generations. They were a proud, insular people, and generally looked down with disdain on anybody that may be working a boat that wasn't from their 'stock'. During the 1939-45 war, the Ministry of Transport decided to recruit women from all walks of life to work on these boats so as to release more men for military duties. It was a steep learning curve and extremely hard work. They did, however, gradually gain the grudging respect of those that had, like so many generations before them, done it all their lives. Susan Woolfitt was to write a fascinating account of her experiences of those times and produced a book called 'Idle Women'.

The book was recognised as the first accurate account of what life was really like on the boats due to the fact that, largely, the boat people couldn't read or write.

One aspect really struck a chord with me. If a 'girl' was to do something different from the norm and a 'boater' witnessed it, subject to the action making sense, they would ask to see the operation again. In other words, despite their incredible expertise, they prided themselves on always being able to learn a different way of doing things if it improved the operation.

On a slightly different note I sometimes forgive myself for not being as competent as others in whatever field, because I've come to the conclusion that a Master is someone who's got it wrong a lot more times than I have.

But still we may have to be ready to face a response from either a critical parent or a rebellious child ego state.

"Yes, I hear what you're saying (about length of service) but don't you think there's a chance that you've been lucky all this time?"

"You'd be pretty angry with yourself if you have to spend your retirement years in a wheelchair/one handed/blind/deaf ".

"The bottom line is this. If you carry on like that and have an accident there'll be a major enquiry. My neck would be on the line as well as yours unless I'd said something."

"You're actions are going to give me nightmares. I couldn't forgive myself if you lose a limb and I hadn't said anything, just for the fear of pissing you off."

You might find these clumsy and no, I wouldn't say these things in this sort of way, but hey, they're just one dimensional variations on a theme.

Being confronted by a big dominant personality can be intimidating. You might be nervous of their ability to make a publicly humiliating joke at your expense. But bear in mind you are more than likely dealing with someone operating from either a critical parent or rebellious child state. If you can maintain a quiet, dignified position from an adult perspective, you'll probably surprise everybody, not least yourself.

Another difficult situation can be when someone is working unsafely in order to speed up the operation. "If we don't get this done today, we'll have to come back tomorrow".

We might respond by pointing out the fact that if they carry on as they are, they, or we, won't be going anywhere tomorrow. If we're lone workers, we might have to point this out to ourselves.

It's dodgy ground and I don't really want to explore this area, but if it stops an accident, you could resort to bending or exaggerating the truth when relating a story that may or may not have happened to a friend or colleague of yours in the past. "Oh, the screaming, the pain," etc. I'll leave that one with you.

It's easier if you're more experienced than the person you feel you need to talk to, but care is still needed if we are to remember that our intention is to improve all aspects of the situation. A rebellious child might continue to operate unsafely just to spite you. We're looking to bring out the adult ego state.

I remember a time when I was working with a small team that were brush cutting around some canal locks in a public area. Everything was in place in the form of method statements, risk assessments, personal protective equipment etc. We had started the job very early to minimise the risk to the public, but no amount of signage stops a determined jogger, cyclist or a dog walker. A relative youngster had joined us. I would describe him as very keen. He'd gone through the brush cutter training course, but was continually breaking one rule - that of not keeping a constant eye out for members of the public. After two close shaves (yes, it should only have been one) I found a way of attracting his attention and approached. I still didn't know what I was going to say until, luckily for me, something popped into my head.

"Do us a favour, George?"
"Whassat?"
"If you see me doing something dangerous would you promise to stop and tell me?"
"Yeah, course"
"OK, I'll go first. We've got to keep a constant eye out for the people that don't know that we can throw a small stone at them at 50mph. It could easily blind one of them and then we're all in the doo doo. We must look out for them every few seconds."

Thankfully, I got a grin and a more vigilant team mate.

There are going to be times when you fail, but at least you tried. If apparent failure is inevitable you're then going to have to decide what to do next. It may be worth remembering that, even if you suspect you're going to be beating your head against a brick wall before you stop an operation, if you can be creative and effective enough, (the operator may well be too proud to modify their behaviour in front of you), the chances are they're going to have a think about, and hopefully act upon, what you've said. Remember that they've got a genius subconscious that's listening to everything you say. Who knows, they may even trot out your lines to someone that's operating unsafely elsewhere in the future.

I can't and never could, get close to your own environment or personal abilities with reference to effective communication and how it might be used in the workplace, but if you could just open your mind, go mad with your imagination, have fun (?).

There might be times when you have been unable to intervene for whatever reason.

You might have been simply too far away.
You were unable to get to the operator.
Words did actually fail you.
You simply couldn't expose yourself to a danger.
It would have been more dangerous to leave your post or stop what you were doing.
Stopping the operation would have made it even more dangerous,

and so on

If you feel that you should have intervened, then there might be a case for an 'after chat'.

After the event, either immediately or soon after (perhaps over a beer), with your adult 'head' on, you could consider asking for a moment of your colleague's time to discuss your concerns. The very fact that you've wanted to voice your opinion in a semi formal way will probably make the operator think about what you're saying. The first response you get might not be the one you would've desired, but there's a good chance that it will be considered.

Whichever ego-state you've encountered when facilitating, remember that you've been talking to somebody's subconscious as well as whatever 'show' they've responded with. The subconscious mind will know that what you've said is right, or that, at the very least, your motives were pure.

# Chapter 7

## *Lone working*

In the main we've looked at working with or around people. Many of us often have to work alone. This situation offers us all sorts of temptations. We can cut corners, ignore rules, ignore good advice or paperwork, largely without fear of interruption.

I'd suggest that, to a point, we've all done it. There are, however, a couple of things we could look at, but for now take another breather.

A few years ago I'd suspected we had a big cat in the area. I'm going to tell the story using one of my 'Lock Keeper Stories'.

~~~

I was getting used to expecting the unexpected. London was loud, busy, sometimes dangerous and intensely varied. But ostensibly sleepy Hanham Lock made London look like the Gobi desert on a quiet Sunday afternoon.

Megan, 'the border collie pup' and I were out on our constitutional one afternoon when I spotted a mink in the river. It swam to the bank and I, growing ever curious about such things, wanted to see if it had a home nearby. Even as an ex-townie I knew I wouldn't find a little front door and a 'Please wipe your feet' doormat, but I hadn't seen a mink residence before. The river was very low, and a little beach had been left at the bottom of the vertical bank. No sign of the mink, but I could clearly see its hoof marks. And alongside, a purposeful, hungry, 'Don't mess with me' set of footprints. These size 14s belonged to a large animal. It had come out of the water, walked along the little beach, and had calmly got back into the river. A domesticated dog would have clambered out, woofed a 'phew', whined and padded about trying to compute loads of excuses not to get back in again, the bank being too steep to climb up. This was something different.

Over the previous couple of weeks there had occurred a series of events that, in isolation, meant nothing. Megan the pup found the hind leg of a deer and wouldn't share. She would normally have nipped the heels of Mike Tyson given half a chance, but on a separate occasion she was found cowering terrified in a corner of the garden after a bit of a barking session. She'd met something big. The carpet in my study started getting squelchy because the cats refused to go out. Trails of blood down the drive; strange and unusual nocturnal noises. I came, nervously and yet excitedly, to the conclusion that we had a big cat in the area.

After a bit of research I discovered that four people I knew had seen a big cat over the last six months, two very recently. I also found out other snippets of information. They liked to hunt mink. If a little river carved through their territory, they'd happily swim it. There are big cats all over the country in the wild, but this was so close to Bristol it could have stood for Mayor. So I had no choice but to do what any full blooded and fearless lock keeper would do. I called for Malcolm.

Malcolm is a curious mixture of somebody Bristol should be terribly proud of while also requiring several stints in a secure unit for the incurable shot potter. Should you ever encounter him in the Lock & Weir Pub, you know you are sitting within feet of enough assorted weaponry to liberate Wales. If his mane of hair shuts like curtains across his steamed up glasses, his shoulders hunching in a camouflage jacket that could only be removed by major surgery, then you know he is dreaming of invading a small to medium size country.

This man will shoot at anything that moves and if it doesn't move, he'll shoot at it until it does. He'd previously lent me an air rifle and being Malcolm's, it had a sniper sight and had been re-bored specifically for taking out police helicopters. It was not an easy decision. I'm talking about a man who goes hunting squirrels with napalm.

Malcolm arrived and climbed out of the turret. He had brought a camera with him and I wasn't at all surprised to see, 'NASA - DO NOT REMOVE' stamped on the side. He was in an eloquent mood.
"Where?"
I took him to the little beach where the prints had by now increased in number.

After what seemed like several hours of light meters, angles and computer programming, he took a photograph and started to pack his things away. One photograph! I'd shot off two reels of film over those wretched prints having borrowed a camera from my mum. Admittedly I'd forgotten to take the lens cap off, but at least I'd made an effort.

"Probably a fox."

A fox!! A measly fox? If it had been a fox it would have been so big we would have been able to see where it had banged its head on some of the lower branches. I called the local newspaper. They took the photograph off me and sent it to the Zoo. I'm still waiting for an answer. A fox indeed! I toyed with the idea of taking Malcolm to the Zoo and show him 38,000 species of fox. But even if he came along lightly armed he would still scare the animals. Curiously enough I haven't seen any sign of the big cat, since Malcolm.

~~~

What relevance has this to lone working? Well, I did my research into big cats in the wild and found out many fascinating facts about them. I have come to the conclusion that they, as well as many other animals like them, are the ultimate lone workers.

Even though any large cat in the UK has probably escaped from a private zoo, they have retained all their natural instincts.

Here's the important bit. They will never do anything, or allow anything, to cause themselves harm. They keep themselves immaculately groomed, claws needle sharp and are amazingly observant. In this example, we (humans) are the potential accident. They'll steer very clear of humans unless we directly threaten them at very close quarters. If they became ill or injured in any way, they would not be able to survive. They keep themselves at the peak of readiness and perfection as much as they possibly can. They have to be able to fulfil their instincts to hunt and breed. We can't compete on that level, but we can try and identify with their ideals.

Wild mink, on the other hand, don't seem to care nearly as much. They're absolutely fearless when it comes to humans. They'll happily knock on your back door, demand a cup of sugar and then bite your charitable finger. If mink could be made aware of Behavioural Safety, they might get together in a big team meeting and say, "Right chaps, we need to find out why we get shot at, a lot. Malcolm who?"

We've all but wiped them out from our neighbourhood.

On a more human level, there are the people that go out with brush cutters etc. to maintain the trails across some of the National Parks in the US. Due to modern technology emergency communications are no longer an issue. That being said, they still plan and prepare for, down to the last detail, what they are going to accomplish in their day ahead. Their equipment is maintained to the highest of standards, their kit is checked down to the tiniest detail. They are individually dropped off in the morning; 'cut' their long stretch and are then picked up again in the evening. If anything should fail, either their equipment or themselves, they would have to walk back and start where they left off. Apparently it's a matter of honour as well as sheer practicality.

I've rather changed my thinking about using dangerous tools. I've come to the conclusion that they're like very poisonous snakes. Yes, they can be handled safely, but they oh <u>so</u> want to bite you if you'll just give them the chance.

We would also do well to take an extra few minutes to think about the implications of doing something hazardous, even if it does save us time. As I mentioned earlier, I have become a lot less 'gung ho' since I became a dad, started looking towards my retirement, as well as quite simply getting fed up with niggling cuts, bruises, aches and pains. There are also times when I force myself to contemplate not being able to work at all and what that would mean to me, my family, and our way of life.

Having said that, not so very long ago I had cause to do some work on an outboard engine. This involved drilling out a piece of metal using a battery drill. The drill bit broke. I removed my safety glasses (smugly employed, because it was my time and not the company's) and attempted to prize out the broken end of the bit. It pinged out straight into my eye, forcing an eye lash into my eye ball.
If only I'd been made aware of the basic tenets of

Behavioural… oh never mind.

It's also interesting to watch people who are extremely adept at their craft, doing the equivalent of a golfing 'air swing' or practice stroke. It's a technique used in almost all sports. This could apply to us when we're using a variety of tools. Going through the motions before a 'cut' or something similar, can show us if we can reach safely, or if it's going to strain a muscle or a tendon etc.

By the same token, how many of us have ever used a fire extinguisher? We see them in our work place, our vehicles, in cinemas, schools, boats etc. It doesn't matter whether you are a chief executive officer or the newest employee, I'd suggest that everyone should pick up a fire extinguisher, feel the weight, look at the operating mechanism, learn how to identify what kind of fires it can be used on, and imagine using it. There might not be anyone around to ask should you need to use it.

Safety equipment surrounds us in many forms. We may or may not have noticed it, so familiar has it become to the background of our daily lives. There are a million different combinations to any given scenario and I've tried so very hard not to keep writing … 'but only you have the ability to turn my own limited examples into your own possible realities', but…we may be on a boat belonging to a friend of ours. The engine fails; we're being blown towards a lee shore or swept towards a weir. The order comes, 'drop anchor'. We're on our own (everyone else is busy panicking, administering first aid etc). We've probably all seen an anchor before, but what if we'd previously gone up to it to see how it worked. Can we lift it without putting our backs out? Where would our feet be positioned?

To grossly exaggerate this point, I remember hearing the story about the jeweller who worked for a diamond company. One of the largest diamonds ever found had been given to him to 'dress'. It took him a whole year of planning and 'practising' with his tools before he struck his first blow. Such was the stress he felt when he finally did it, he fainted!

I do believe, regardless of our 'lone' activity, it is well worth consciously thinking about the basics of why method statements and risk assessments exist. Whether it be clearing out a pond, hiking, para-gliding, pumping out a flooded cricket pavilion etc, and all the other things we might get up to both in and outside our working lives, the approach should be the same.

Identify the hazard.
Quantify the risk.
Minimise the risk.
How and from where help might be sought.
Who knows where we are, what we're doing, and how long we're likely to be doing it?

Some very bright people have been discovered crushed under their cars after a jack has failed; asphyxiated in cricket pavilions; drowned at the bottom of garden wells; dead from hypothermia on hill sides; crushed under collapsed walls; drowned in caves; incinerated in their garden sheds; face down in gaseous mud etc.

There are literally millions of such tragic cases, but hey, it's never going to happen to us (?).

# Chapter 8

## *Conclusions and miscellaneous aspects of Behavioural Safety*

Very obviously I couldn't even attempt to go into job or activity planning because nobody has the ability to write a book on 'planning for every eventuality under all circumstances for everybody'. Even if anybody were remotely qualified it would be a great waste of effort and rain forest, and would be largely wrong and meaningless to most people. I'm also just as sure that there are already many 'activity specific' books covering many subjects closer to (your) home. The point I'm trying to make is that we could perhaps look at our own way of approaching a task or activity and be prepared to change our thinking. For instance, how do we assess a danger? What can we use more effectively when trying to gather 'data'?

The River Avon responds quickly to heavy rainfall and boat owners can end up in all sorts of difficulties. This sometimes requires me to hastily assemble a team of 'rescuers'. Apart from going through the obvious planning stages, there are two things I will always say or ask them.

Firstly, I will ask them for all their ideas on what things could go wrong, the worst that could happen, and what we could do to be ready for such events.

The other thing I always suggest is the fact that no-one can be all seeing and all knowing and any member of the team, however inexperienced, is to point out anything they might spot as being potentially hazardous. I tend to paraphrase this by saying 'no question is too stupid, no observation too trivial'. I think it focuses everyone's minds as well as making everyone feeling vital and included.

In an industrial or commercial context exit strategies should have been catered for. But something I'd learned on a chainsaw course for example, is, when you park your vehicle, which way is it pointing? If you wanted to leave in a hurry, perhaps with an injured person on board, is the vehicle ready to go? If you're injured but have to get your chunky vehicle to a place where help can be sought, are you going to have to do a fifty point turn?

We can take this further still. Have the seats that you may need to use got cluttered in the excitement of going off to your activity? Are the keys handy? The list could go on and it's not something anybody can comprehensibly write about. I'm suggesting that none of these things require any extra effort, just a slight change in thinking because you'd have to turn the vehicle around anyway. You're just doing it sooner rather than later because you never know what might happen.

On that same chainsaw course we all had to take it in turns to be the team leader. Every morning one of the first jobs of the team leader was to ask every other member of the team, by name, if they were feeling physically and mentally up to the day's activity. I think this is another good 'focusing' technique.

There are situations where you may have to go against some rules. For example, if you need to pull a car out of a canal or up a steep bank and the only cable you have is damaged or 'hockled' (kinked), do you still continue with the job? If it's not a life or death situation then maybe not. If it is, then you have to know and quantify the dangers.

We may come across a situation where, if we were to follow the paperwork or regulations to the letter, our activity may become dangerous. Again, we have to assess the dangers and modify our plans (we're rigidly keeping to the speed limit but the all consuming mud slide is catching us up).

I'm going to repeat something I included in an earlier chapter.

How important is Behavioural Safety?

Much more important than any risk assessment, method statement, training course, proudly maintained personal protective equipment, a sign with big large red letters saying 'Thou shalt not'...

All of the above can be in place and they exist for a reason. At the pink end of the scale, they are there to inform, protect, educate and warn. Somebody has had to try and out think and subsequently engineer out, any potential bad happening.

If one were to be cynical, they are there so that someone can say "but all the paperwork was in order". The bottom line is they mean absolutely nothing (until a court of enquiry) if our behaviour is not up to the mark.

There are some that believe every single accident is preventable. I want to agree with them, but, try as I might, I find I can't. Those same people would suggest that a plane downed by terrorists is preventable (yes, but historically, who pissed who off first?) in the same way that a broken glass bottle on a beach is preventable (yes, but it used to have a message in it saying 'Help, I'm marooned on a desert island'). We live in a world of falling rocks, blood clots, metal casting defects, inclement weather, equipment failure on a molecular level, cleverly concealed poisonous snakes, wasps that fly in and want to criticize our driving, tsunamis etc.

We can enjoy this dangerous and exciting world of ours with a much greater degree of safety if we:

1) Vastly increase our observation of potential hazards, whether it's new, or has been staring us in the face for years. It could be large and obvious, it might be small and deadly. It might even be us who are the hazard.

2) Minimize the risk of a hazard occurring or reaching its full potential while we still can by intervening or

reacting. Reducing the risk also involves minimising the effects of, or being ready to deal with, an accident.

3) Increase our ability to communicate effectively to pre empt, cease or solve, educate or inspire.

A team of Waterways 'Policemen' were out on their launch on the River Thames. The engine faltered and slowly died. They restarted the engine out of gear and all was fine. The action of putting it in gear to set off, however, caused the engine to fail again. They came to the conclusion that they had something around the propeller. The boat had a 'weed hatch' which is set into the hull over the propeller and is designed for one to be able to remove anything that might be fouling the prop. One of them removed the weed hatch cover and found several yards of rope wrapped firmly around the prop and shaft. He found that by tugging on the rope and turning the prop at the same time he could gradually unravel the rope. Noticing the exertions of their colleague, the others went back to help him. Their extra weight at the back of the boat caused it to tip and water started to come up through the weed hatch. Because so much rope was now inside the boat, but also still firmly attached under the water, they were unable to put the lid of the weed hatch on and the boat quickly sank. Next time they would all be aware of the danger, as now we all are. (Sorry, Ray, but the image of peak caps on red faces spiralling down the River Thames was too good not to tell).

Were we to map the concept of Behavioural Safety in its purest form on to this scenario, we could start with the paper work.

A risk assessment and method statement had been completed. These included what the activity involved, the hazards, minimising the risks (drowning, by the provision of life jackets, adequate training etc). A 'point of work' risk assessment (a book of blank forms) had also been carried out by the team when they arrived at the boat. Up to this point, the responsibility has been at an organisational or employer level.

Then we get to the (Behavioural Safety) nitty gritty.

There was a change in conditions. This could have been a hundred different situations, some of which may have been catered for in the risk assessment.

With the benefit of hindsight, in the case of exposing the weed hatch, if there had been the briefest of team consultations, the danger of a few large policemen all moving to one end of the boat, might have been identified. The closing scenes of 'The Italian Job' spring to mind.

Most importantly we live in a world where a chain of events that lead to an accident can be simple or complex. Some sequences we can spot, others would run into so many permutations that we may as well stop having children and wrap ourselves in cotton wool. Between these contradictions (and on first reading, this book may apparently contain many) there is a happy safe medium.

I didn't know whether to laugh or cry when I read about the woman who was driving her shiny new RV down a freeway. She decided to activate the cruise control before going back to make a cup of tea. The Judge awarded her one million dollars in compensation after finding the sales company guilty of negligence. Oh for goodness sake!! When we all decide to hold our hands up and be responsible for our own actions there might be a lot more money sloshing around for those that really need it. Lawyers will just have to find another way to stay rich.

Additionally, all the planning and paperwork in the world can't cater for how our outside world can sometimes interfere with our minds. Can someone operate a potentially dangerous piece of machinery if their minds are preoccupied by a divorce/money worries/subtle or obtuse bullying/teenage kid problems/being in love/in a hurry for own purposes/in a hurry for someone else's purposes? Well, yes, largely, but many accidents are caused because our minds are 'not on the job'.

I know the arguments will always rage on when it comes to blanket site regulations, I'm only suggesting that, from top to bottom, we all need to realise that a safe head is safer than a safe hat, because a safe head will know when to wear one.

My friend Paul works on houses that have been newly built. After all the big construction toys have been put back in their box, his job is to go and lay the type of floors that we see in the sales brochures. He thoroughly resents working inside these houses (the construction of which has been strictly controlled by building regulations) with a hard hat on. It makes for very uncomfortable working, especially on a hot day. If, however, he was caught without one (inside the house), he would be fired off the site without any level of discussion. There again, his shiny new house might be a target for a plane load of terrorists, in which case the regulations would have been spot on.

On the other side of the coin, a few years ago, a father and son team were using a tractor and flail to cut the hedges along a canal side towpath. It was a one man job, in a single seat cab. They'd found out, however, that it was much quicker if one drives the tractor and one operates the flail. To further speed up the job, instead of going the extra distance to turn round, they opted for a fifty point turn where they'd finished the job. The tractor went into the canal. They couldn't get out through the 'vandal proof' escape door, and tragically, paid the ultimate price. At the very end survival instinct versus love must have played a part.

All the paperwork was in order.


Observation, intervention, communication.

Lightning Source UK Ltd.
Milton Keynes UK
26 February 2011

168272UK00006B/12/P